AMERICA
Online.

Wired in a Week

AMERICA
Online.

Wired in a Week

How AOL Can
Improve Your Life in
**10 Minutes
a Day!**

Regina Lewis

AOL's Online Advisor

WARNER BOOKS

A Time Warner Company

Copyright © 2000 by America Online, Inc.
All rights reserved.

Warner Books, Inc. 1271 Avenue of the Americas,
New York, NY 10020
Visit our Web site at www.twbookmark.com

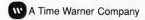 A Time Warner Company

Printed in the United States of America

First Printing: November 2000

10 9 8 7 6 5 4 3 2 1

ISBN: 0-446-67736-1

PCN: 00-191162

Book design and text composition by H. Roberts Design

Acknowledgments

● ●

This book emerged from conversations with AOL members—in schools and hair salons, on planes and in taxis, at grocery stores and family reunions.

Thank you to everyone who shared stories about AOL with the talkative blond woman toting two children who asked, "So, you on AOL?" Turns out, if you listen well—and we pride ourselves on that at AOL—the book practically writes itself. But, of course, it doesn't end up on paper and in print that effortlessly. For that, there are many to thank. . . .

Thank you from the bottom of my heart to my wonderful family. Thank you Steve Case, Bob Pittman and Ted Leonsis for being more inspiring than you can imagine. Thank you, Jonathan Sacks, for making the first phone call. Thank you, Larry

v

Kirshbaum, for taking it. Thank you, Jonathan Edson, Jim Bankoff, Les Pockell, and Amy Einhorn, for taking it from there. Thank you, David Seldin, for the writing, Jesse Kornbluth for the editing, and Melissa Stirling for everything in between. Thank you, Annie Brackbill, and Wendy Goldberg, for the votes of confidence, and Jan Brandt for your guidance. Thank you, Marshall Cohen and team, for the research. Thank you, Jeff Kimball and team, for a great product, and Joe Hall for all his help. Thank you, Philip Fleet and the thousands of AOL customer service representatives who help AOL members all day, every day, and know more about the AOL service than any "Advisor" ever could. Thank you, Heather Perram, for your support from the start, and Joe Redling and Bob Potter for the promotional muscle. There are so many others. Thanks to everyone involved in producing what we hope will be a valuable resource for AOL members. Most of all, thank you, Caroline Teasdale, for making all of the above happen with such grace and determination.

Contents

● ● ● ● ● ● ● ● ● ● ● ● ● ● ● ● ● ● ● ●

Contents

 Introduction

"It's like learning to learning to ride a bicycle."

1

 **Remember when you learned to ride a** bike? You were scared at first and very shaky. Glad to have someone at your side to get you going. But once you got the feeling and your balance, you couldn't be stopped!

Getting online is like learning to ride a bicycle. I can see you now . . . whipping off a quick e-mail to a friend . . . checking the latest news, sports, and weather online . . . planning a vacation and scoring the best deals available in cyberspace.

And if you're feeling reluctant, know you're not the only one:

"I wouldn't even know where to begin."

"I never had a computer, and I don't understand them anyway."

"I'm worried about my kids being safe online."

"I'm too old to learn."

"I'm afraid I could hurt my computer."

I know you can do it, because I've gotten my grandmothers, my parents, aunts, uncles, cousins, friends, and neighbors online. Some were hesitant, but once they were "wired," they all said the same thing we hear every day from AOL members: "Wow, this is easier than I thought!"

There's no excuse anymore for not getting online.

Thousands of people are overcoming their concerns each day and making the Internet part of their everyday lives. There are now more than 116 million "wired" Americans, with that number continuing to skyrocket.

And our research shows that Internet users— once a concentrated group—are increasingly people just like you. Men and women. Young and old. And from every corner of the world, every walk of life, and every profession. There was probably someone standing by their side as they got started who gave them a little push. Think of me as that person and this book as that boost.

I hear some of you saying, "I'm already online. What does this book offer me?" There's plenty here for you as well. For starters, the AOL disk contains the latest version of our software— AOL 6.0—which is easier and more convenient to use than ever. So you can upgrade your software, learn about some of the new features it offers, and maybe even pick up a few additional pointers to help you get even more out of your AOL experience. I myself discover new areas and shortcuts on AOL every day, and you will too, once you know where to look.

Changing Your Life. In Just Seven Days!

Like millions of people, you'll soon discover some of the life-changing benefits of being on AOL.

We'll start with learning about e-mail—the fastest, easiest, and most convenient way to keep in touch with friends and relatives. There are more than 335 million exchanged daily—once you start communicating via e-mail, you'll never go back.

And that's just scratching the surface of the benefits of AOL.

This week:

☞ You'll learn how to save time and money online.

☞ You'll check the news, weather and sports scores.

☞ You'll chat with friends, family and celebrities.

☞ You'll take advantage of online personal health and finance resources.

☞ You'll find out how to ensure a safe and enjoyable online experience for your children.

☞ You'll discover how AOL can make your life easier and more convenient.

This and much, much more, along with Insider Tips and Hi-Wired activities if you're more advanced or as you become more advanced. Your online experience is what you make of it, so let's begin.

 ## What Is AOL?

AOL is an "Internet online service." It consists of two parts:

☞ An Internet Service Provider (ISP)—your seamless connection to the Internet (sometimes called the World Wide Web).

☞ Exclusive AOL tools and features such as e-mail and content conveniently organized for AOL members.

AOL is a "gated community" in the vast and sometimes daunting World Wide Web universe, which is growing exponentially. In 1999 there were 3,649,000 unique Web sites on the World Wide Web. An average of 4,222 new sites launch every day. AOL tames and edits this rapidly exploding universe, making the Wild West of the Web as familiar as the streets of your neighborhood. Because whether you're driving a car or a computer mouse, it's nice to know where you're coming from and going to.

 ## Let's Do It!

If you've got a computer, a phone line/jack, a modem (or other connection device), and this book, you've got everything you need. Give us a week and we'll have you "wired" in less than 10 minutes a day. The clock is ticking, so let's get going!

DAY 1

Get Started!

 *An important note: Everything that follows* in this book is based on the latest version of our software, AOL 6.0. If you're using an older version of the software, some of the things we talk about may be different. We encourage everyone to upgrade to AOL 6.0 using the same process we describe here for installing AOL the first time.

A Word About You: If you have this book, we're assuming you're either a) an AOL member who wants to know and do more online, or b) someone who wants to become an AOL member. If you're an existing member and are already using AOL 6.0, you can give the CD to a friend and skip ahead to Day 2. For everyone else, let's start at the beginning, with six easy steps to get your online life underway.

Step One: Get Your Computer "Wired":
After your computer is unpacked and assembled, you need to hook up your modem to a phone line. Your modem is the part of your computer that enables you to access the Internet. If you have Internet connections through your cable service, or high-speed connections called DSL, your cable provider or phone company has already hooked up your connection to the Internet. If you have a Macintosh computer, some—but not all—of this book will be relevant.

The modems on most computers connect to the Internet through the same type of jack and cord that connect your phone to the wall. Consult your computer manual to find the modem connection on your computer and plug the phone cord into it. Plug the other end into an available phone jack in the wall. You may need to unplug a phone line to free up a jack and reconnect your phone when you're not online. If you have two phone lines, use the second line for your computer.

 Step Two: Learn To Use The "Mouse": Almost all computers come with a mouse. It's either an oval device connected by a cord to your desktop computer or a ball and pad on a laptop. The mouse allows you to control the computer by clicking one of the buttons on the mouse—usually the left button.

You need to look at your computer manual to learn how to plug in and use your mouse. If your computer is on and your hand is on the mouse, you can roll the mouse around on a flat surface. You might also want to use a mouse pad—a little place mat designed to provide extra traction and control. As you roll the mouse around, you'll see a small symbol, usually an arrow, move around your screen. This symbol is known as a "cursor." You can use the mouse to move the cursor around the screen, which will enable you to take advantage of all the great features available on AOL.

Step Three: Install The Software: Now it's time to put the AOL 6.0 CD into your computer so you can sign up for membership. Turn on your computer and insert the AOL CD into the CD-ROM drive on your computer. Your computer will automatically "open" the AOL installation program. Again, if you're already an AOL member, you can use the CD to upgrade to version 6.0, or give it to a friend. The upgrade process is free and takes a matter of minutes. As soon as you insert the CD, your computer will go through a series of steps. First, the AOL installation screen will come up on your screen, asking you to click on one box (also referred to as a "button") if you are a new member and another if you are a current member. Click on the appropriate one, and we're on our way.

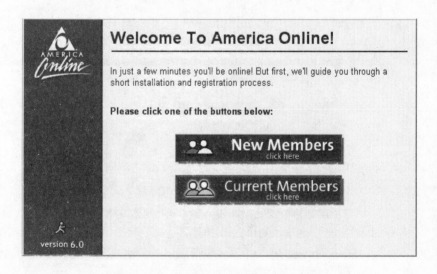

As the installation process proceeds, you will periodically be asked to click "Next" to approve what the software is doing and move on to the next step. Clicking "Next" at each step will result in a safe, successful installation. When in doubt, click "Next."

Step Four: Choose An Access Number:
After proceeding through a few screens, you will come to a new page where you will be asked to select the phone number that AOL will use to connect you to the Internet. You will first be asked to enter your area code, so the system can locate access numbers in your area. Type it in and click "Next." If you have call waiting, you will be prompted to select a special calling option so incoming calls will not interrupt your online connection. You'll also be asked to indicate if you need to dial 9 to reach an outside line. From there, click "Next" again and your computer will connect to AOL for the first time.

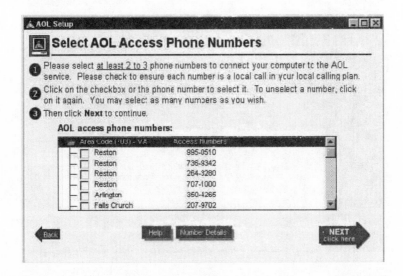

You'll hear a sustained honking sound that lasts a few seconds. This sound tells you the modem is working. (You should hear it every time you connect to AOL.) Soon you'll see a list of the available access numbers in your area. Review the list and choose the number that is closest to you. Once you have chosen a number, click on it once to select it. You will see a red check mark appear. If available, choose at least two local phone numbers. If you're not certain which numbers are local calls for you, check with your phone company to be sure. Then click "Next" again, and move on to the next step.

Step Five: Register Your Account: After you've finished setting up your access numbers, it's time to register for your AOL account. You'll be asked to type in the registration number and password found on the AOL CD.

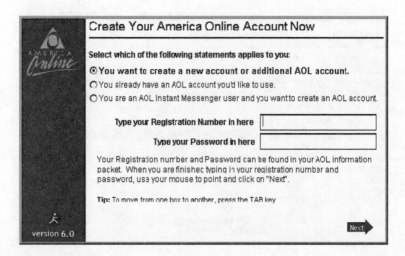

Then you'll be asked to enter your name,
address, and billing information, including the
credit card or checking account number you
want to use for your new subscription. (Remember, you won't be charged a monthly fee during
your trial time.) This information is strictly confidential, and we use the most advanced cutting-
edge technology available to protect your privacy.
Importantly, AOL has the highest standards for
privacy and security of any online service
provider and will never give out your credit card
number or any other personal, demographic, or
financial information. You will also be asked to
accept AOL's Terms of Service agreement
designed to help ensure a safe and secure experience for all AOL members. We ask all new members to agree to adhere to AOL's Community
Guidelines. It's all part of taking pride in and pro-
tecting the AOL community and includes treating
other AOL members with respect and avoiding
vulgar or hurtful language. Thanks in advance for
doing your part.

Step Six: Pick A Screen Name And Password:
This final step sets the stage for your cyberspace
debut. It's time to pick your AOL screen name
and password. Your screen name will be your e-
mail address, the one you give out to family and
friends, so consider choosing a name that is easy
for you to remember and for friends to recognize.

It can combine letters, numbers, and blank spaces. Screen names are a bit like vanity license plates, so be creative. If you want to be businesslike, it can be an initial and your last name. America Online has more than 23 million members. Many utilize multiple screen names—you get seven with each membership—so don't be surprised if your first choice is taken. You may be given alternative suggestions or asked to try another combination if you don't get the screen name you'd like right away. Keep experimenting, and you're likely to find one that's available and works for you, especially since AOL screen names can now be up to 16 characters long.

After you've chosen your screen name, it's time to choose a password. This should be a combination of letters and numbers. Consider it as confidential as your ATM bankcard PIN or other secret codes.

That's it. You've done it! Your online experience will now begin with what just may be the four most famous words in cyberspace: "Welcome! You've Got Mail!" We will automatically take you to the AOL "Welcome Screen," which gives you access to the most popular page in cyberspace, with favorite AOL content and features. The Welcome Screen changes daily, as do many of the visuals throughout AOL. That's why some of the illustrations in this book will not look exactly as they do on your computer screen. Our chairman, Steve Case, sends a welcome message to all new members. In Day 2, you'll learn how to check this message and read Steve's greeting.

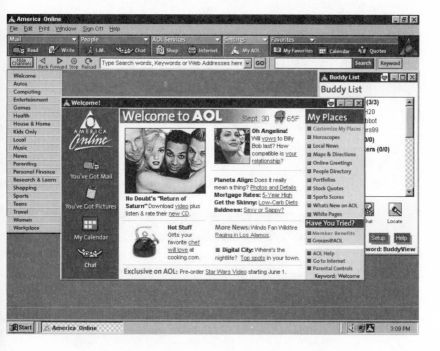

If you have time, explore a little bit. Use the mouse to click on a few things on the screen. There are no "mistakes" when you're exploring online and you can't hurt anything, so don't feel intimidated. When you're done looking around, click your cursor on the words "Sign Off" on the "toolbar"—the rulerlike box at the top of the screen. A "pulldown menu" will appear. Move

your cursor down to the words "Sign Off" on the "pulldown menu," and click again. You'll hear the word "Good-bye" and know your session is over. The Sign Off/Sign On screen will appear.

CONGRATULATIONS! You've successfully signed on—and off. Nice start! Get ready for tomorrow by calling a few close friends or family members who you know are online and ask for their e-mail addresses.

INSIDER TIPS

→ Write down your password—soon you'll know it like the back of your hand, but for now it's best to write it down and keep it tucked away somewhere safe.

→ While we've asked for 10 minutes a day, getting a friend who's already on AOL to show you around can save time and make the online experience even more rewarding right from the start.

→ You can sign on to AOL from any computer that has AOL installed on it. Just click on the arrow on the right-hand side and scroll down to "Guest." Sign on, and, when asked, enter your screen name and password. (You can also access your e-mail on the Internet at www.aol.com.)

DAY 2

Get in Touch

 *I always meant to write letters and call old* friends more. Now it's so quick and easy to craft messages online, I'm in touch with the people I care about most all the time. I honestly think I'm a better wife, mother, daughter, sister, and friend since I've been online.

I'm not alone in finding it easier to stay in touch online. Every day, AOL delivers millions of e-mails and even more instant messages. As for group conversations, there are more than 16,000 chats daily on America Online. From pregnancy to pets to personal finance, you name it—they're talking about it on AOL.

There are three basic ways to communicate with family, friends and colleagues and meet new people online: e-mail, instant messaging, and chatting.

E-Mail—
Electronic Mail

E-mail (electronic mail) has totally revolutionized the way people communicate with one another, making it simpler than ever to stay in touch. Consider the great advantages of e-mail:

- ☞ It's free.
- ☞ Messages can be short or long.
- ☞ You can send e-mail to more than one person at a time.
- ☞ You can send e-mail around the world in just seconds.
- ☞ You can read e-mail whenever it's most convenient.
- ☞ You can attach pictures and documents.

Instant Messaging—
Lives Up to Its Name!

Instant messages are just what they sound like. You write a message, press "Send," and your note pops up on the other person's computer screen— right away—in a little box that looks like this:

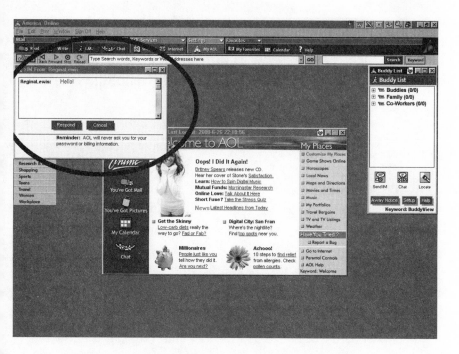

Instant messages let you carry on a conversation online just as quickly and easily as you could with a person sitting across the table. You can "IM"— it's pronounced "eye-em" and is the nickname for instant messaging—with a friend while you check sports scores, look for movie listings, or do anything else online. It's best to keep IMs short. Longer messages are better suited for e-mail.

Chat/Message Boards—
Express Your Thoughts

If you like meeting new people and expressing your thoughts and opinions, then a chat room is the place for you. AOL hosts thousands of chat rooms on topics from politics to parenting as well as support groups of all kinds. You're virtually guaranteed to find a chat room where people share your interests.

Chatting moves quickly, so if you'd prefer to take your time expressing your opinion or reading what others have to say, check out the message boards. Message boards are similar to chat rooms,

Families Channel Message Boards	
Families: Click twice on a message board community to read messages posted by other members or share your own thoughts.	

Topics	Subjects
News For Families	69
Dads Message Boards	16
Tell Us Your Immigration Story	4
Parenting	5
Pregnancy Circles	28
Single Parenting	16
Entertainment	10
Family Issues	40
Adoption & Fostering Message Boards	8
Homeschooling Message Boards	2
Scouting Online Message Boards	6

List All   List Unread   Mark Read   More   Subscribe   Find by...

ABOUT MESSAGE BOARDS | PREFERENCES | HELP |

but the conversation doesn't take place in "real time." Throughout AOL you'll come across opportunities to review and contribute to message boards, which is like "posting" a message on a bulletin board.

Let's Do It

Sending E-Mail

Do you have e-mail addresses of family and friends? Write them on a Post-it note and attach it to your computer for now. Let's start by sending e-mail to someone whose address you know. Log on to AOL by clicking on the AOL icon on our main computer screen and then typing in your screen name and password in the provided space and clicking "Sign On."

Now click your mouse on the "Write" paper-and-pencil icon on the AOL toolbar—located at the top of the screen —the second icon from the left. 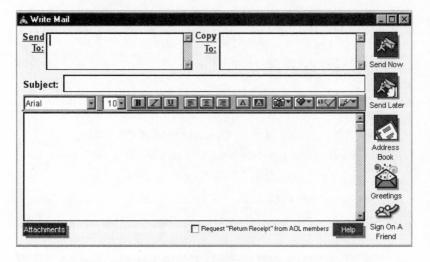 An e-mail screen like the one below will appear.

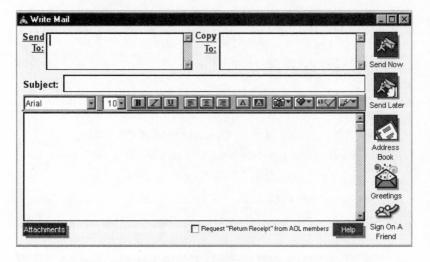

If you do not have someone's e-mail address or if you just want to try it out, send an e-mail to yourself. Since you're on AOL, there's no need to include the "@aol.com" part of your address. If you're writing to someone who's not an AOL member, you need to type in their entire Internet address, including the "@" sign and the part following it, which usually ends in .com or .net (e.g., jsmith@mars.com).

When the blank e-mail form appears, your cursor will be in the "Send To" box. Then type in one of the addresses from your list.

Want to send mail to more than one AOL member at a time? In that case, just put a comma after the first e-mail address, add the second, and continue like this:

When you're done addressing your letter, move on to the "Subject" box either by hitting the "Tab" key twice or by clicking your mouse any-where in the "Subject" box. What you type here will appear in the recipient's e-mail inbox, along with your e-mail address, so that they can tell whom the message is from and what it's about. For now, just type "Hello."

Now we're ready to move on to the main body of the message. Move your cursor to the large box at the bottom of the e-mail form, either by clicking your mouse there or hitting "Tab" on the keyboard. Then type away. A good message for now might be "This is my new e-mail address. I'm wired!!!!! Please write back. Bye for now." Your e-mail should now look like this:

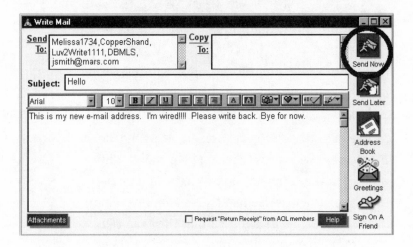

When you're finished writing and checking your message, click the "Send Now" button in the top right corner of the e-mail form. A box will pop up saying it has been sent. Click on the "OK" button.

If you're like most AOL members, this will likely be the first of many e-mails you'll send and receive.

HOW DO YOU KNOW IF SOMEONE READ THE MAIL? Click on the word "Mail" from the first column on the toolbar. Select "Sent Mail" from the pulldown menu.

Then highlight the item of mail in the "Sent Mail" listing and click on the "Status" box at the bottom of the screen. If the mail was sent and opened by an AOL member, you will see the date and time it was read. If it's not yet been read, it will simply say "not read yet." This feature does not work for mail sent to non-AOL members.

Receiving and Responding to E-Mail

Most AOL members log on several times a week and spend an average of over an hour a day online, so it probably won't take long before one or more of your recipients writes back. In the meantime, you'll get a message from our Chairman Steve Case, welcoming you to America

Online. You'll know you've got an e-mail when you hear the three little words you'll soon come to love—"You've Got Mail"—coming from your computer speakers. At the same time, the mailbox icon at the far left of the AOL tool bar will change to show the red letter flag icon standing up.

Empty Mailbox   **"You've Got Mail!"**

To read your mail, click on the mailbox icon, and your e-mail inbox will appear. If you have more than one message waiting, it will look like this:

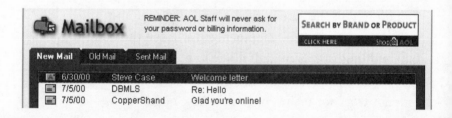

Double-click on the message you want to read, and the e-mail form will come up. After you read the message, you can easily send your reply. Click on the "Reply" button at the top right corner of the e-mail and a new e-mail form will appear, with the "Send To" and "Subject" boxes already filled out. (*Note:* If you received a note that was sent to more than one person and you want to reply to the entire group, click on "Reply All" instead of "Reply.")

Type in your message and send it, just like a new e-mail, and it will instantly appear in others' e-mail boxes.

Instant Messaging

Setting Up Your Buddy List

Now that you're getting the hang of e-mail, it's time to move on to instant messaging. The first step is to set up your "Buddy List," which

will let you know when your online friends—
your "buddies"—are online at the same time
you are.

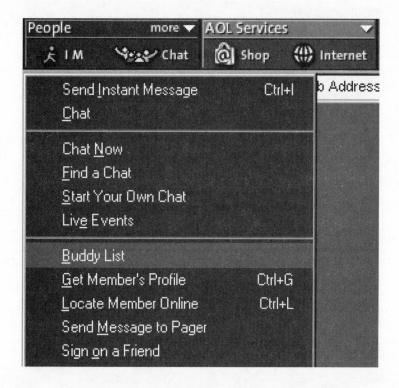

If your Buddy List is not up on your screen
now, you can bring it up by clicking on the "People" icon on the toolbar. Select "Buddy List."

Your Buddy List will pop up on the screen.
Before it is set up, it looks like this:

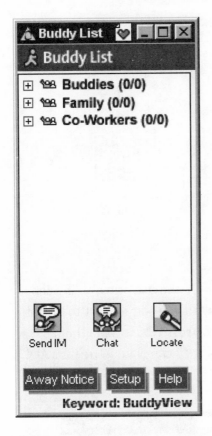

To start entering your buddies, click on the "Setup" button at the bottom of the "Buddy List" window. Another window will pop up, showing three "folders" in which you can place your buddies. For now, use only the "Buddies" folder. Click the "Add Buddy" button at the bottom to enter it.

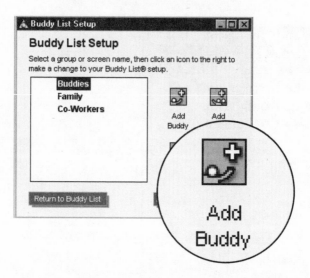

If you have friends who use other online services, they can IM with you—at no cost to either of you. **Go to Keyword: AIM** to send them information on how they can sign up free for AOL Instant Messenger.

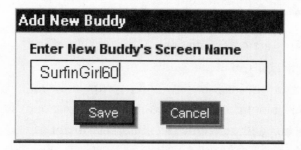

Enter your buddy's AOL screen name, click the "Save" button, and he/she will be added to the list. Repeat the process with the next name.

When you are done entering buddies, click the "Return To Buddy List" button at the bottom left of the window.

You will most likely notice that some of the screen names you entered don't appear on the list. That is because not all of those people are online right now. Only those buddies who are currently online will show up on your list, so you know they're available to receive instant messages.

If a screen name on your Buddy List is in parentheses—like this: (ReginaLewis)—your buddy just signed off. If it has an asterisk next to it—like this: ReginaLewis*—he or she just signed on. The numbers in parentheses at the top of the list tell you how many buddies you have, and how many are currently online. If it says (3/10), that means that you have a total of 10 buddies, and that three of them are currently online.

When you want to let people know you've stepped away from your computer, click on the "Away Notice" button on your Buddy List. This feature will let people know why you're not responding to instant messages.

Sending and Receiving Instant Messages

Now that you have your Buddy List set up, you're ready to enter the world of instant messaging. If you end up doing one thing online more than any other, this might just be it.

Choose one of your buddies who is online, or
call a friend and tell them to log on. Click once on
their screen name, and then click the "IM" button
at the bottom of the Buddy List (you can save time
by simply double-clicking on their screen name).
An instant message form like this will appear.

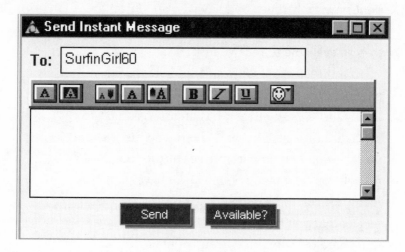

Your cursor will already be in the larger box at
the bottom of the form. Type a quick message
and click the "Send" button. It's that simple. Your
buddy's computer will make a quick bell sound to
let them know he/she has a message, and your IM
will appear on their screen. Sometimes people
might not answer your instant message instantly;
they may have stepped away from their computer.
That's why so many instant messages begin with
"Are you there?"

Now you can keep going back and forth as
long as you like. As you are typing on the bottom
half of the window, the text appears only on your
screen. When you click the "Send" button, it will
be added to the top half of the window on both
screens. You can read back through the text of
the entire conversation using the up and down
arrows at the right side of the window.

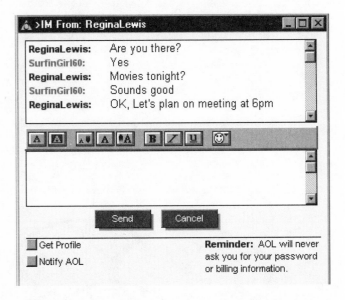

Instant messaging is so popular it's spawned a
language all its own. Here are some fun, short
phrases and symbols you can use again and again:

☞ AYT—Are you there?

☞ G2G—Got to go

☞ CYA—See Ya

☞ AFK—Away from keyboard

☞ BRB—Be right back

☞ BAK—Back at keyboard

☞ LOL—Laughing out loud

☞ ROFL—Rolling on the floor, laughing

☞ IMHO—In my humble opinion

☞ IMNSHO—In my not so humble opinion

☞ BTW—By the way

☞ GMTA—Great minds think alike

☞ :)—smile

☞ ;)—wink

☞ :(—frown

☞ {}—hug

☞ :*—kiss

Chatting

If you want to use the online world to meet new people who share your interests, then it's time to hit the chat rooms, one of the most popular activities on AOL.

The first step is to find a chat interest by going to People Connection, AOL's home for chat. To get there, click on the "Chat" icon on the toolbar.

This will take you to the People Connection, which looks like this:

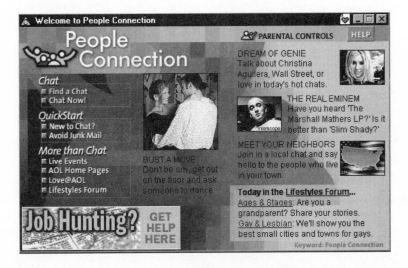

To search through the list of active chats, click on "Find a Chat" at the left side of the screen. This will bring you to a menu of the available chats.

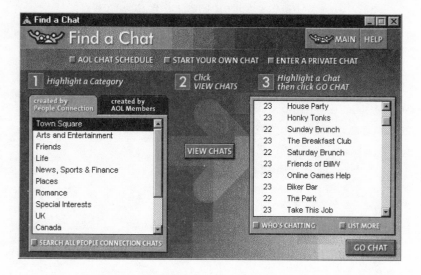

Look through the list of categories on the left-hand side of the window and highlight one that interests you by clicking on it once. Then click the "View Chats" button in the middle of the screen and a list of chats in that area will appear in the right-hand side of the screen.

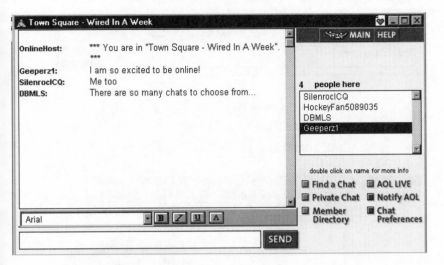

The chat room window has three main parts. The largest box is the area where the chat is actually going on. It's usually a good idea to follow the conversation for a little while before jumping right in so you can see what people are talking about. The box along the right-hand side of the window shows a list of people who are currently in the room.

When ready to participate in the chat, click on the box at the bottom of the screen to put your cursor there and then type what you'd like to say. When you're finished typing, click the "Send" button and your message will appear as part of the chat. Everyone who has entered this room will be able to see what you have written after you push the "Send" button.

To leave a chat room, click the "X" at the top right corner of the window to close it. The "Find a Chat" menu will be visible.

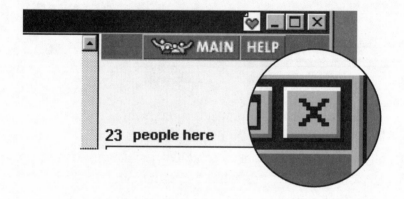

Note: Because chat rooms are public forums, as in any public place there are all kinds of people and you never know who you're going to run into. The good news is, when you're online, you have the control. If you are in a chat room and someone is bothering you, you can double-click on their name and select "Ignore Member." You will no longer see messages from that member.

As for incoming instant messages and e-mails that annoy you, a smart response is to delete them and not write back. Like unsolicited junk mail you receive in your U.S. postal mailbox, junk e-mail can pile up. For more tips on curbing unwanted e-mail—including setting up a separate screen name for chat—go to "Mail" on the toolbar and select "Mail Controls" on the pulldown menu.

INSIDER TIPS

→ Spell-checking your e-mail is as easy as A, B, C. Click on the icon: [ABC✓] before sending.

→ Some of the most powerful chat and support groups online are formed around health and relationship issues where members share common experiences and foster close-knit groups.

→ The more you're online, the more e-mail addresses you'll likely want to keep track of. Just add them to your online address book—go to "Mail" on the toolbar and select "Address Book" from the pulldown menu or click on the "Address Book" on the side of AOL e-mail.

If you're really on a roll, here's something extra you can do on AOL.

→ If you like instant messaging and chatting, you might want to chat privately with a group of invited guests through AOL's Buddy Chat and Private Chats.

Hi-Wired 1

With AOL 6.0, there are now all kinds of new, free ways to give the next e-mail you send some personality. Go to Mail Center on the AOL Toolbar for these and other options:

☞ **Color.** Mix and match more than 48 color choices for e-mail typefaces and backgrounds. You can even customize your own colors. Blue type, yellow background . . . the combinations are limitless.

☞ *Writing style.* Your handwriting isn't like everyone else's and your e-mail writing style doesn't have to be either. With AOL 6.0, you can now choose from more than 100 font choices and 16 point sizes—everything from casual to formal and from big to small.

☞ *Accent.* Put some punch in your point by bolding, italicizing, and underlining words. Or use all three at once. **B** *I* <u>U</u>

☞ *Mail art.* Want to send flowers, a birthday cake, seashells, or a kiss? Take your pick; it's free. Bring your e-mail to a whole new level with these easy-to-add images and sounds. Click on the "Mail" icon on the toolbar and select "Mail Extras" from the drop-down menu. Check out all the cool stuff you can add to your e-mail!

☞ *Hyperlinks.* If there's something online you'd love to share, send a direct "link." Just click and drag the heart icon from the upper right corner of the screen into the message you are writing. And voilà, a blue hyperlink will instantly appear in your e-mail, allowing the recipient simply to click on the link and go directly to that site or feature.

Getting Help Online

It's bound to happen. Sometimes you just need help, especially when trying things for the first time. AOL prides itself on being easy to use and that means making sure help is always free and accessible—online and offline.

Fortunately, on AOL help is literally only a click away. Where to click? Simple—anywhere it says "Help"—at the right-hand side of the toolbar, on the bottom of your e-mail screen at **Keyword: Help** (more on Keywords in Chapter 2), and wherever else indicated. From there, you'll see

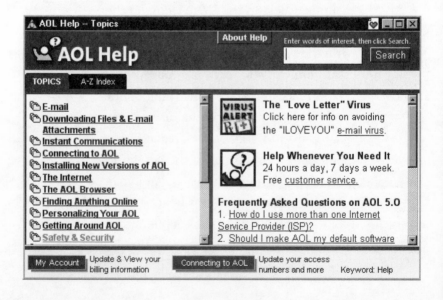

various help topics of interest with links to step-
by-step instructions.

Online help resources are great for novice and
advance computer users alike, not only for solving
problems, but also for learning more about AOL.
You'll be amazed how many different things you
can find out how to do just by clicking on different help topics. Popular topics and frequently
asked questions include: downloading files and e-
mail attachments and "How Can I Recover E-Mail
I Recently Deleted?"

One of the best things about getting online
help is—if you only have one phone line—you
don't have to log off to call for help on the telephone. You can even get free, one-on-one customer support via e-mail.

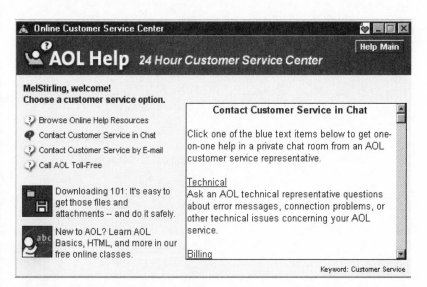

Of course, if you'd prefer to talk with someone, you can always call our customer service centers toll free, 24 hours a day, seven days a week at 1-800-901-9795. But you'll find it's often much quicker and easier simply to check the online help section first. You can even update and view your AOL account billing information online—it's fast, easy, and secure.

DAY 3

Get the Info

 *I begin each day by reviewing the AOL Welcome* Screen, scanning the headlines, and checking the weather and my horoscope. By the time I'm through with my morning coffee, I feel "connected."

That's the glory of the Internet: You can find what you want, when you want it. AOL makes finding the best of the best on the Internet easy.

What Can You Find?

☞ Online versions of newspapers and magazines.
☞ All the information you need to manage your health, finances, and daily life.
☞ Local weather, television, and movie listings.

☞ Up-to-date dictionaries, encyclopedias, and atlases.

☞ From cars to colleges . . . You name it, there's something about it online.

By design there are several ways to navigate AOL, just as there are several routes from your home to your job or school. Don't be surprised when multiple paths take you to the same place.

Let's Do It

The Welcome Screen

As you've already discovered, every time you log on to AOL, two windows come up right away—1.) the Welcome Screen, and 2.) the Channel Menu (and your Buddy List if you set it up on Day 2). Think of these two together as being like the lobby of a building—it's a short step from there to anywhere you want to go.

The Channel Menu appears along the left-hand side and is your guide to all of the content available on the AOL service. Using your mouse, move the pointer slowly down the column, without clicking anything. As you pass over each button, a "hint text" will appear, explaining which topics the channel contains.

Click on any one of the channel buttons and you'll go directly to that exclusive AOL area. No matter what channel you pick, you'll quickly find there's lots more behind this screen. Let's look around.

The Channel Menu will stay on your screen wherever you're online, unless you choose to close it by clicking the "Hide Channels" button. When you're finished looking at a channel, just click on the "X" in the top right corner of the channel screen.

The other component of the AOL "lobby" is the Welcome Screen, which will fill most of the space on your screen when you log on. This is divided into three main sections.

On the left-hand side of the screen are three icons that connect you to popular AOL features described in other chapters of this book—e-mail, My Pictures, My Calendar, and chat.

To the right of that section is the biggest part of the Welcome Screen, highlighting some of the most interesting and popular content available on AOL that day. These listings change frequently— several times a day as you log on and off—so it's

worth checking them often. You'll notice that
there are many items in this section that are
underlined and in blue letters. Each of these is a
"link." Clicking your mouse on a link will connect
you to the content described.

When you've finished looking at that page, click the "X" at the top right corner of it to close the new window, and you'll be back at the Welcome Screen.

Many people think the far right hand side of the Welcome Screen is the most helpful. It highlights some of the most popular areas. Click on anything you see and you'll be directly linked to some of AOL's premier content. You can personalize this column by clicking "Customize My Places." This will allow you to put some of the AOL content that's most important to you on the Welcome Screen.

There are three basic ways to get the information you want on AOL: Keywords, Channels, and Search.

AOL Keywords: One of the most popular
things about AOL is the easy-to-use Keywords
that make it incredibly simple to find your way
around online. To get to a particular area on
AOL, or to many sites on the Internet, you can
just use one word or a simple phrase—such as
"Sports" or "News" instead of a long Web
address with lots of "www"s and "colon, backslash, backslash."

If you know the AOL Keyword for the area
you want to visit (they are often mentioned in
advertisements for various Web sites and are
included on the bottom of AOL screens) just follow three quick steps:

☞ First, click on the "Keyword" button on the
right-hand side of the AOL toolbar. A small
"Keyword" box will appear.

☞ Second, type the word or phrase into the
"Enter Word(s)" space in the "Keyword" box.
☞ Third, click the "Go" button, and you'll be
connected to the corresponding area.

Doesn't that sound easy? Try it now with the **Keyword: Wired in a Week**.

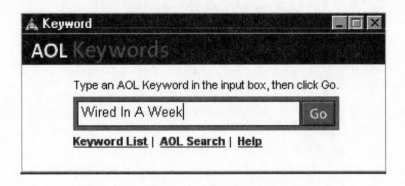

You can ignore spaces and capitalization when you use keywords, so Wired In a Week will work as well as wiredinaweek.

If you don't know the appropriate Keyword, there are a couple of things you can try. First, in the "Keyword" box, next to the "Go" button is a button labeled "Keyword List." Click it to see a full list of thousands of AOL Keywords.

You can also try just entering a word that you think might work as a Keyword. You'll be surprised how often it works. If you're looking for help with your income tax returns, for example, try **Keyword: Taxes,** and you'll find all kinds of help.

If the word or phrase you type isn't recognized as a Keyword, then the system will treat it as a search request (more on those in just a second), so you're one step ahead of the game.

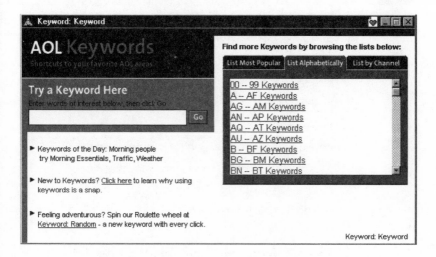

Popular Keywords

Here are some of the most popular AOL Keywords:

- ☞ Local
- ☞ Love
- ☞ Shop
- ☞ Pets
- ☞ Baby
- ☞ Movies
- ☞ Sports
- ☞ Finance
- ☞ Kids
- ☞ Dictionary
- ☞ Faxes

☞ **Recipes**
☞ **Weather**
☞ **Horoscope**
☞ **Health**
☞ **Help**
☞ **Auctions**
☞ And, if you can't decide which of AOL's areas you'd like to visit or just want to experiment, try **Keyword**: Random and we'll pick for you.

Your Guide to the Channel Menu: Want to find out if your favorite team won last night? Go to the Sports channel. When you click on any of these buttons, you will be taken to that channel's main screen. Each channel is set up differently, but they all highlight the most interesting and up-to-date information and connections to more information on various related topics. AOL channels include: Auto, Computing, Entertainment, Games, Health, House & Home, Kids Only, Local, Music, News, Parenting, Personal Finance, Research & Learn, Shopping, Sports, Teens, Travel, Women, and Work & Careers.

On the Parenting channel main screen, for example, you'll find a few news headlines relating to family and child-rearing issues. There is also a menu offering links to more specific information organized by children's ages: pregnancy, toddlers,

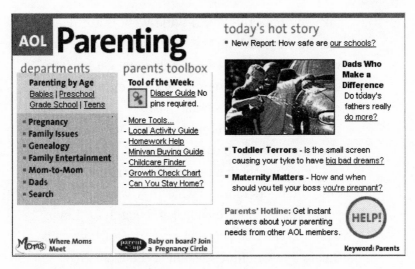

preschoolers, grade schoolers, middle schoolers, and high schoolers.

Finding information on any of the channels is a simple process—when you see something that looks interesting, click on it and a new window will open up with the information you've asked for. There will probably be other links on the new screen to additional things you might want to explore. When you're done with a particular window, close it by clicking the "X" in its top right corner.

This is what people mean when they talk about "surfing." It's just clicking on things that look interesting, and seeing where they take you. With AOL, you never have to worry about getting "lost." Some of the links you click will go to content created by AOL or one of our partners, others will take you onto the World Wide Web. But it doesn't matter. Just click on the "X" to close each window when you're done with it, and you'll get back to the main channel menu, or go to **Keyword: Welcome** to get back to home base.

The best way to find out what AOL's exclusive channels offer is to explore.

Our channel lineup changes periodically to offer members more of what they want, so keep your eyes open for changes and watch for Keywords in the bottom right corner of AOL screens. Spend a few minutes scanning the main pages of each channel. Some of the mainstays of our programming are:

News channel. AOL's News channel, the #1 destination for news and information in cyberspace, features continuously updated news stories each day from a variety of leading news providers, including NPR, the *New York Times*, *TIME*, and CBS. With a continued focus on member interactivity, AOL News has become a national sounding board for conversation and a hub for current event debates and discussions. **Keyword: News.**

Entertainment channel. An up-to-the minute source for information on the latest, most talked-about movies, TV shows, music, and books. The Entertainment channel gives you a variety of ways

to keep track of your favorite celebrities and all of
the entertainment news from sources such as E!
Online, *Entertainment Weekly*, MTV, *People*, and
more. **Keyword: Entertainment.**

Health channel. Nothing is more important than your health, and this channel gives you all the information, tools, sources, and support groups you need to have more control over your own well-being. On the Health channel, you can research health questions, communicate with health care professionals, participate in chat rooms and message boards about a variety of health-related issues, and even order prescriptions. **Keyword: Health.**

Personal Finance channel. Personal Finance gives you the tools to track stocks, research companies, and follow your own portfolio. It also provides tools to help you pay your bills, track your household budget, and calculate your taxes. **Keyword: Personal Finance.**

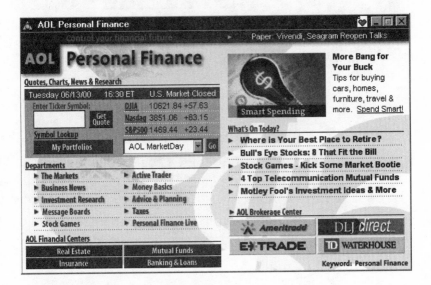

Sports channel. Get the latest scores, injury reports, features, and more. You can follow any professional sports team, participate in fantasy sports leagues, and much more on the best sports site around. **Keyword: Sports.**

 ## Using AOL Search

Sometimes you're trying to find something online in a hurry, and you aren't sure where to look for it. If you can't figure out what channel it would be under and you don't know the Keyword, does that mean you're out of luck? Not at all. AOL Search is a fast, efficient way to find what you want.

The best way to search is:

☞ Click the "Search" button on the AOL toolbar, near the top right corner of your computer screen, or **Keyword: Search.**

A new window will open up with the AOL
Search main screen in it.

Your cursor will automatically appear in the
empty box at the top of the screen. Type what
you are looking for and then click the "Search"
button next to that box.

Depending on what you're looking for, it
might take a few seconds or more. When the
search is completed, you'll see a page with information divided into as many as three categories:
Recommended Sites, Matching Categories, and
Matching Sites. Not all search requests will pro-
duce all three categories.

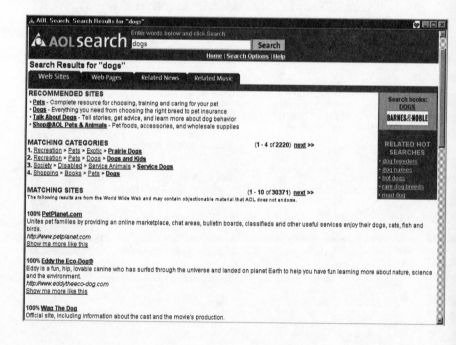

☞ *Recommended.* These are sites that are most likely to be what you are looking for. Click on the underlined blue text and you'll be connected to a site that should be relevant and helpful.

☞ *Matching Categories.* This section contains connections to additional lists of sites that may contain relevant information. Click on any of the categories listed to find additional sites.

☞ *Matching Sites.* This section will list sites that match or come close to matching your search request. The higher up on the list a site is, the more likely it is to be what you're looking for. *Note:* The matching site results are from the World Wide Web and may contain objectionable material that AOL does not endorse.

When you connect to sites using Search, it's important to know that you won't go back to the Search Results page if you click on the "X" in the upper right-hand corner of the screen. Instead, you can go backward using the backward arrow button ◀ on your AOL toolbar.

To experiment, search for the word "President." One of the options returned to you is the official Web site for the White House, where you can find transcripts of all of the president's state-

ments. Search "Lasagna" and find a long list of
matching sites with different recipes. And an "Aus-
tralia" search yields all kinds of interesting info.

In addition to the main AOL Search feature,
you'll find specific search functions on a lot of the
AOL channels, such as Computing and Shopping.
These work pretty much the same way, but they
search only within that subject area. They can be
a really convenient tool for finding something in a
hurry.

INSIDER TIPS

➔ It's easy to be a newsmaker on AOL by participating in one of
the daily polls. You'll see them highlighted throughout the service. Most ask three to five questions and take just a few
moments. So feel free to weigh in.

➔ AOL is constantly updating and improving its content offerings.
Look around when you log on to see what's new or go to **Keyword: What's New.**

➔ The AOL logo in the upper right corner of the screen shimmers
when a search is underway. If you want to stop a search, click
on the [Stop] circle on the toolbar.

Time Savers

For most of us, nothing is
ever convenient enough.
When we first got a
microwave oven, I couldn't
believe how fast it was.
But before long, I got
impatient having to wait
four minutes for the
popcorn to be done.
That's one of the great
things about AOL: Over

time, you'll discover tricks to make your online
experience even more convenient. Even people
who've been online for years are sometimes surprised when they learn some of these shortcuts:

Mark your favorite places. When
you see a Web site you think you might want to
return to, don't worry about remembering its
address or where you found the link to it—just
click on the heart symbol at the top right corner of
the window that site is in, then click "Add to
Favorite Places." The next time you want to visit
that site, go to the Favorite Places menu on the
toolbar and click on that page.

Send online greeting cards. It's never been easier to recognize special occasions. Just go to **Keyword: Greetings** to see a large selection of e-cards for any holiday or event. Choose the one you want, enter the recipient's name and yours to personalize the card, enter the e-mail address you want it sent to, and voilà— instant greetings, without any trips to the store or the post office.

Use AOL News Profiles. Instead of searching all over cyberspace for news stories, or worrying that you might miss something of interest, let AOL take care of it. Go to **Keyword: News Profiles** and follow the step-by-step directions there so you can receive a daily, tailored news report via e-mail with the information you need and want the most. It's free and it's a great way to stay on top of specific company, sports, medical or local news.

Research products online. If you're making a major purchase such as a house, car, furniture or appliances, or deciding which brand of car seat you want to get your child, you can save a lot of fact-finding time and plenty of headaches by starting your search online. Look through Shop@AOL (**ShoppingSearch**) and use the exclusive AOL "Search" function.

Find a job. There are hundreds of thousands of résumés and job listings posted online. So whether you're an employer or an employee, go to **Keyword: Jobs.**

Learn online shortcuts. It doesn't seem like a big deal, but there are a lot of computer "shortcuts" that can save you a second here and there. After a while, those seconds start to add up.

☞ If you hold down the "Control" button on your keyboard and press "K," the Keyword window will pop up.

☞ If you're trying to find a particular e-mail in your inbox, hit "Control" and "F" for find, then enter the sender's screen name and it will be located.

☞ If you press the "Control" button and "M," a blank e-mail form will appear, ready for you to address, write, and send.

There are lots more. Click on the toolbar menus and look for "Ctrl+" after some items to learn the most often used keyboard shortcuts.

DAY 4

Get the Goods

 **If you love to shop, you'll soon come to agree**
the Internet is the best invention
since the mall. Once you get a taste
of how easy it is to shop online with
Shop@AOL, you'll come back again and again.
You can shop any time of day or night from the
comfort of your home or while you're at work.
You can even shop in your pajamas! And because
AOL has millions of members, we're able to use
that buying power to negotiate some of the best
deals in cyberspace—or anywhere else.

Shopping is one of the fastest-growing online
activities. Take a look at just a few of the advantages of shopping on AOL:

☞ You'll never have to "fight the crowds" at the mall, find a parking space, or worry about getting a last minute gift.

☞ AOL has a huge selection of high-quality products and great values, so good that experts have called Shop@AOL the "Internet's Miracle Mile."

☞ AOL's 100% Guarantee of Satisfaction and Security takes the worry out of buying online. **Keyword: Guarantee.**

☞ There's no more dragging packages from the store to the car, and from the car into the house. Products ordered online are delivered right to your doorstep, or wherever else you'd like.

☞ Shop@AOL makes it incredibly easy to find what you're looking for—search by item, merchant, and/or price, making comparison shopping a breeze.

It doesn't matter whether you're buying a frying pan for $15 or video camera for $1,500—shopping online is simple, fun, and easy. Apparel, jewelry, home furnishings, gourmet foods, toys, books, cosmetics, flowers—you name it, it's available online.

And, again, if you're making a major purchase like a house, car, furniture, or appliance—or if you're deciding which car seat to buy for your new baby—you can save a lot of research time and make informed choices by starting your search online. You'll be amazed at all the useful consumer information you can find and how easy it is to find it.

Let's Do It

 Shop@AOL

Some people would like to shop online, but they just don't know where to start. On AOL, that's not a problem. Use the Channel Menu to go to the Shopping channel, click on the shop icon on the AOL toolbar, or enter Keyword: Shop, and there you are. You'll see that AOL has done all the legwork. We've pulled together the best of the best to create an amazing one-stop shopping destination—Shop@AOL.

The first thing you'll notice will likely be the "featured promotion." Every day, companies make special offers to AOL members. A lot of the discounts can be incredible. If something catches your eye and you want to take advantage of it or find out more, click on the item and you'll connect to the appropriate department.

The heart of the Shop@AOL main page is the

menu of product categories. As you can see, there is a wide range of shopping categories available. Click on any one of these to see a more detailed menu of departments, along with links to particular stores, more features and special offers.

This makes it easy to see what online shopping sites are available in these categories and where you might find something you're looking for.

If you know what you're looking for, there's an easier way to find it. Shop@AOL's search feature helps you find just the right item. This feature can be found on the Shop@AOL main screen and at the top of each department page is a bar that looks like the regular Search bar.

Shopping Search

Type in a brand or product

sweater

search

It works the same way, except that the results you get will be a selection of items from our shopping partners that match the word you entered. Give it a try with "sweater" as an example.

Once you've found the product you want, it's time to try making a purchase. Each site works slightly differently, but they all follow the same basic principles. Just follow these easy steps:

☞ When the item you want to purchase is on your screen, look for a button that says "Add to shopping cart," "Purchase," or something similar. Click on it.

Buy it Now!

Add To Cart

Add this item to your shopping cart.
You can always remove it later.

☞ Your shopping cart will display the item you've selected. You can either go back to shopping for other items to add to your cart or click "Proceed to checkout."

☞ You'll then be presented with a form to fill
out, asking for your name, shipping address,
and other information, along with your credit
card number. All of the participating merchants have met stringent criteria and use
cutting-edge secure technology (see "AOL's
Certified Merchant Guarantee" below).

If you're buying an item to send as a gift, you'll
also be able to enter the appropriate name and
address and even text to have printed on a gift card.

Select a payment method.

Credit Card

○ American Express
○ MasterCard
○ Discover
◉ Visa
○ Diners Club
○ JCB
☐ This is a Purchasing
Card

Credit Card Number

Expiration Date
06 ▼   2000 ▼

☞ You will be given a last chance to change your choices or decide not to make the purchase. If you want to go ahead, click "OK" or "YES."

Please be sure to click this button.

☞ Your credit card will be charged, and the product will delivered to your house, or to the recipient of your gift. The site will e-mail you a confirmation notice/receipt. It's a good idea to print this out and save it until the product arrives.

That's all there is to it.

AOL's Certified Merchant Guarantee

AOL guarantees your satisfaction, security, and privacy—total satisfaction. **Keyword: Guarantee**.

For your protection, all AOL Certified Merchants offer return policies backed by AOL's money-back guarantee. If, for any reason, you are not satisfied with your purchase, you can contact the merchant through the store's Customer Service area. If, after contacting the merchant, you do not get a satisfactory resolution consistent with the store's posted customer service polices, you can outline your complaint and notify our Shop@AOL Help Desk. We will intervene on your behalf to assist you in obtaining full satisfaction from the merchant. Should any AOL Certified Merchant not comply with its return policy as stated in the merchant's Customer Service area, then AOL will provide you a refund for the full purchase price.

AOL Protects You

Every time you shop with any of AOL's Certified Merchants, you are protected against liability in the unlikely event of credit card fraud; simply follow your credit card company's reporting procedure. AOL will reimburse you up to $50 for any remaining liability for unauthorized charges. AOL offers a level of safety and security not available at your local mall.

Since the creation of AOL's shopping area and the inception of our Guarantee in October 1996, the Shopping channel has never received a report of a credit card that was compromised during a shopping transaction with Certified Merchants on AOL. Our commitment to our members is to maintain this record by providing you with advanced, up-to-date security technology.

Security

How does AOL make shopping online so safe? AOL helps to protect you from transaction fraud by making sure all AOL merchants provide a secure and safe environment for credit card purchases. When you make a purchase through AOL, the information you provide is scrambled.

As a result, in the highly unlikely event that an unauthorized person intercepts the transmission, he/she won't be able to read or to understand any of your personal information. For your convenience and safety, AOL automatically provides you with built-in scrambling technology (known as a secure browser) if you are using AOL 6.0, 5.0, or 4.0. For others, there's more information about upgrading your browser at **Keyword: Browser**.

Never Give Out Your Password!

Protect yourself from credit card fraud by following this simple guideline: NEVER give your credit card information or password to unauthorized persons contacting you via e-mail or instant message. These requests are *always* fraudulent, however clever or compelling they may sound. For tips on identifying official AOL Mail, go to **Keyword: Official AOL Mail.** Bottom line: The only times you will be asked for your credit card number will be during initial AOL registration, when making a purchase online, or when changing your AOL payment to a new credit card at our free 24-hour online billing center. Otherwise, AOL or its affiliates will never ask you for your credit card number or your AOL password via e-mail or instant message.

INSIDER TIPS

→ Take advantage of free gift wrapping and shipping specials.

→ Use the same password for shopping sites that ask you to "register" and use the same one for all shopping sites so you don't forget it.

→ If you're looking for a pet or just want to find out more about them, going online might be your best bet. It's estimated that hundreds of pets are adopted via AOL each week. **Keyword: Pets.**

→ Consider online gift certificates, which can be used at top retailers online and emailed right away. A lifesaver for last-minute shoppers. **Keyword: Gift Certificates.**

→ Consider giving an AOL membership to someone you'd like to keep in touch with throughout the year. A unique stocking stuffer, Mother/Father's Day and Birthday gift idea. **Keyword: Friend.**

Hi-Wired: Online Auctions

Do you like garage sales? Have something special you collect that you're always on the lookout for? Do you consider yourself a professional bargain hunter? If you answered yes to any of these, then online auctions are the place for you.

You may have heard of ebay, the online auction house. Go to **Keyword: Auctions** to get there on AOL. Basically, it works like this: Someone decides to sell an item and places a notice on the service. People who want it enter their bids. You can check back to see if someone has outbid you and decide if you're willing to offer a higher price. At some point, after a set amount of time has passed or the seller is satisfied with the price, the auction is closed, and the highest bidder wins. It's fun, and a great way to get hold of hard-to-find items.

Money Savers

AOL offers some great online values. In fact, if you play your cards right, most months you can save enough to pay for your subscription. Here are a few places to start:

Join the Insider Savings Club. Shopping online can be a great way to save a few bucks. In addition to the online specials AOL offers and the chance to compare prices using the Shopping search feature— you can get additional savings by joining the AOL Insider Savings Club. To sign up, go to **Keyword: Insider Savings**. Click on the button that says "Subscribe." There you go: You're signed up and eligible for hundreds of dollars in savings every month. Each month, you'll receive an exclusive AOL Member newsletter alerting you to special deals on favorite items such as CDs, books, health and fitness items, furniture, clothing, and more. Joining is absolutely free.

Sign on a friend. Here's the deal. If you sign up a friend for AOL, you'll not only get another name to add to your Buddy List, you'll get cash as well! Not a bad deal. Just go to **Keyword: Friend** and enter your friend or relative's name and address. We'll send them a free AOL CD. If they use the CD to join AOL and stick with the service, you'll be rewarded.

Stay in touch with e-mail and instant messages. Sure, you often want to hear your friend or family member's voice, but if you talk to someone regularly on the phone, try chatting online half or even one quarter of the time.

Clip coupons online. You know the coupon circulars in the newspaper? They're online too, and with one click, you can print the ones you want. Go to **Keyword: Coupons** and you may find great savings at stores in your area every week.

Stop paying for out-of-town news. A lot of people who've moved away from the place they grew up or lived for many years still subscribe to the hometown paper to keep up with what's going on. This is often expensive. With AOL, you can most likely read the paper online, and save on out-of-town subscriptions and postage rates. Perform a search for the newspaper's name to get its Web site.

Use AOL/AAdvantage miles. AOL and American Airlines have teamed up to offer the best rewards program around. You can earn and spend miles both online and off, saving all kinds of money on everything from airline tickets to magazine subscriptions. Go to **Keyword: Advantage** to find out more. Additional travel bargains can be found on AOL's travel channel. **Keyword: Travel**.

AOL membership perks. Because so many people have joined AOL, we're able to negotiate special deals for our members on a wide range of products and services. Check in regularly at **Keyword: Perks** for the latest.

Trading stocks online. If you invest in the stock market, you probably know how trading fees can take a bite out of your profits (not to mention what they can do to your losses). But as with so many things, you can find great savings online. Check out the various online trading services on the AOL Personal Finance channel, and you might find a more profitable way to invest. **Keyword: Finance**.

Look for special bargains when you log on. Sometimes when you log on to AOL, the first thing you see will be a special offer for AOL members from one of America Online's e-commerce partners. These exclusive opportunities for everything from credit cards to computer software to digital cameras are often some of the best bargains available anywhere. Check them out and save.

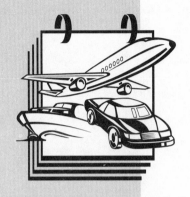

DAY 5

Get Going

Finding your way around online can make it faster to find your way around offline. My husband—like most men—never stops to ask for directions, but now he always uses Mapquest to print directions for the fastest route to wherever we're headed. **Keyword: Maps**.

Around the corner or across the globe . . . to the movies or the museum . . . to the diner or dentist. Booking travel, getting directions, buying tickets, and tracking down local events, shopping, jobs, and attractions. You can do it all online.

Let's Do It!

Time to Travel

The AOL Travel channel is one of the most popular e-commerce destination on AOL—and no wonder. From its main page, you can plan a trip and book flights, hotels, rental cars, or cruises.

Let's give it a try . . . by searching for a flight. On the main screen, click on the "Plane" icon. Then click the box that says "Continue." You'll be asked, "How flexible are your travel plans?" This helps pinpoint the best travel times and fares. Answer the question by clicking on one of the boxes.

Step 1 of 2 | **How flexible are your travel plans?**

⦿ **Very flexible**
I'll plan my trip around the dates when I can get the best fare.

◯ **Somewhat flexible**
I need to travel on specific dates, but I'm flexible about flight times.

◯ **Not flexible**
I need to travel on specific dates and times--I'll build my own itinerary.

Continue ►

You'll see a screen offering you boxes for your departure and destination cities or airports. If you are not sure what the name of the closest airport

---

▣ Shop-Safe Guarantee from Travelocity

Plans: Very Flexible

Step 2 of 2 | **Enter your trip details.***

powered by:

Travelocity.com
A Sabre Company

What type of trip are you taking?

⦿ Round Trip   ◯ One-way

Where do you want to go? (e.g., Dallas or DFW)

Leaving from: Dallas

Going to: New York

Search for the closest airport

How many people are traveling?

Total number of travelers: 1 ▾   How many are aged 2-11? 0 ▾

Find Flights ►

is, you can look it up by clicking on the link to your right. Fill in the city names (no states or countries needed). Select the number of travelers and the number of children traveling and click "Find Flights."

The next screen will give you a selection of the lowest published fares. Select an airline and the following screen will allow you to select your departure date based on availability. Click on the date when you want to depart and then the date when you want to return.

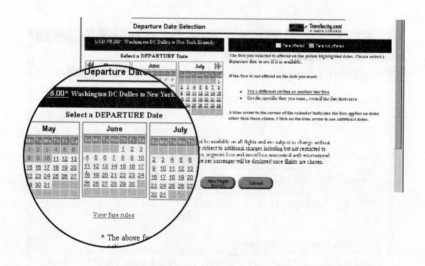

You'll see an array of flight options at the best available prices!

Find a Restaurant on Digital City

It couldn't be easier to find the right place to dine. Simply type in **Keyword: Local** and select a city.

When the main screen for your local version of Digital City comes up, look in the box in the upper left-hand corner and click on the word "Dining." There are many ways to choose a

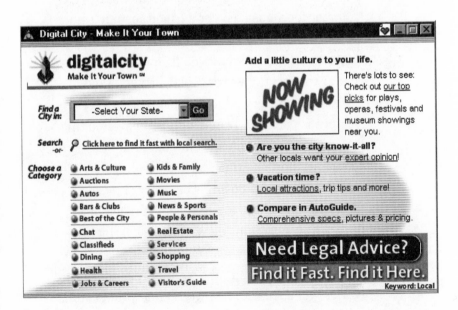

digitalcity
Make It Your Town ℠

Find a City in: -Select Your State-   ▾   Go

Search   🔍 Click here to find it fast with local search.
-or-

Choose a Category

- Arts & Culture
- Auctions
- Autos
- Bars & Clubs
- Best of the City
- Chat
- Classifieds
- Dining
- Health
- Jobs & Careers

- Kids & Family
- Movies
- Music
- News & Sports
- People & Personals
- Real Estate
- Services
- Shopping
- Travel
- Visitor's Guide

Add a little culture to your life.

NOW SHOWING

There's lots to see: Check out our top picks for plays, operas, festivals and museum showings near you.

● **Are you the city know-it-all?**
Other locals want your expert opinion!

● **Vacation time?**
Local attractions, trip tips and more!

● **Compare in AutoGuide.**
Comprehensive specs, pictures & pricing.

Need Legal Advice?
Find it Fast. Find it Here.

Keyword: Local

location, but let's choose "Find a Restaurant" in the box to the left. On screen will appear two choices: "Choose a Cuisine" and "Choose a Neighborhood." Click on the down arrows to pick your favorite cuisine and the area of choice and then click "Go." Look especially for the restaurants with "Pick" in the margin, as this indicates a favorable rating from visitors. If you click on the name, you'll find reviews and an address. And beneath the address, you'll find a map. Now you're ready to go to town—literally!

Find a Number in the Yellow Pages

Throw out your phone book. Finding the number for a business (or a friend) couldn't be simpler online. On the toolbar, you'll see the word "People." Click on it and you'll get a pulldown menu and see the words "Yellow Pages" (and "White Pages" as well for people searches). This feature is particularly helpful if you have multiple phone lines and can use your computer and phone at the same time.

Enter either a business category (I picked "Party Supplies" for my trial) or the name of a business you already know. Enter a nearby town and click on the down arrow to choose the state name. Click on "Find" and a list of related categories will appear to help you refine your search.

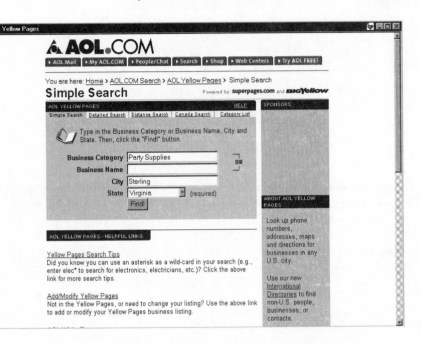

Each category page provides specific listings with telephone numbers.

Find a Movie

AOL has made this simpler than ever. Simply enter **Keyword: Movies** and you'll go straight to our Movies area. On the left side, you can find a

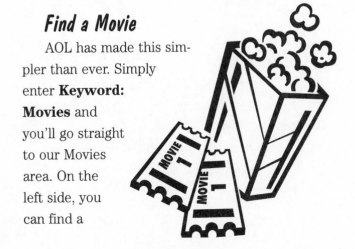

Movie by Name, Browse by Category, by Area, or by Recent Releases. Or you can get Showtimes and Tickets at the top right of the screen. Let's try that. Clicking on this link will take you to AOL's Moviefone. Type in your Zip code and how you would like to search (by theater or by city and state.)

Get Directions

No more worrying about stopping at a gas station to ask the way. Before you go, go to **Keyword: Directions** and you'll be brought to Mapquest, where they'll do all the legwork for you. Then just enter the address information for your starting and ending points.

Maps & Directions

Powered by [illegible]

| Driving Directions | Map an Address | City and Regional Maps | State and Country Maps |

United States & Canada

Where do you want to go? Enter as much of the address as you know.

FROM:

Street address/intersection:

`65465 Dace Drive`

(Or, if address is unknown:)

--select a location--

City:

`Ruckersville`

State/Province:

`Virginia`

Zip/Postal Code:

`25496`

Country:

`United States`

TO:

Street address/intersection:

`1600 Pennsylvania Avenue`

(Or, if address is unknown:)

--select a location--

City:

`Washington`

State/Province:

`District of Columbia`

Zip/Postal Code:

`20500`

Country:

`United States`

Get directions

You can choose door-to-door or city-to-city directions, then click "Get directions." You'll get a map and exact, step-by-step printable directions with mileage.

INSIDER TIPS

→ If you really want the "inside scoop" on a city, there's no better way than to ask the people who live there. Go to Digital City at **Keyword: Local.**

→ Use Mapquest (Keyword: Directions) to get directions from the airport or office to your house and save them so when guests visit or you're planning a get-together at your home, you can easily pull up, print, and forward them by mail or e-mail

→ If you're worried about long lines for the new movie opening this week in a major city, consider purchasing your tickets online in advance. There's no extra charge. **Keyword: Movies.**

Hi-Wired

My Calendar

From soccer games to dentist appointments and from area concerts to TV specials, AOL's My Calendar is a great way to keep your life in order. Go there by clicking the "My Calendar" icon on the Welcome Screen:

To learn more, click the "Tour and Help" tab at the very top of the calendar screen. You can also go to **Keyword: Calendar**.

DAY 6

Get a Life

Sometimes you just want to have a little fun. Fortunately there are all sorts of great online activities.

Whatever you like to do, chances are you'll find something enjoyable when you log on. From games to music and horoscopes to Hollywood gossip . . . .There's something for everyone. You may even meet that special someone.

Once you get going, having fun online is as easy as turning on the television or shuffling a deck of cards.

Let's Do It

Check Your Horoscope

Checking horoscopes is an online favorite and it couldn't be easier. Even if you don't believe in astrology or take it with a grain of salt, there's something about getting a little bit of tailored advice with a few clicks of the mouse that makes for a fun daily ritual. Just go to **Keyword: Horoscope.**

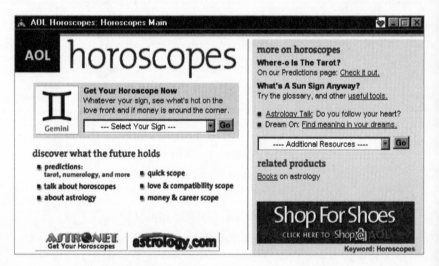

Gossip

Who can resist taking a few minutes to catch up on who said what to whom, and what they were wearing. AOL is a great place to get the latest scoop.

Go to **Keyword: Gossip** for up-to-the-minute info from some of the best sources around.

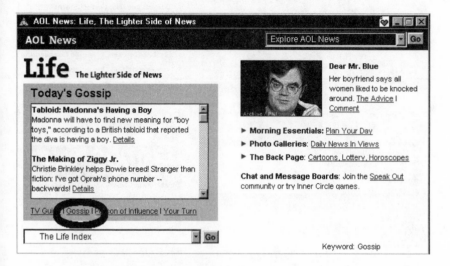

Live Celebrity Chats

Did you ever imagine that you could sit down with a famous person and ask a few questions? On AOL, you can.

Every day, some of the most powerful, famous, and interesting people in the world come by our AOL Live chat room to take questions from AOL members like you. Every major candidate in the 2000 presidential election did a chat on AOL Live. So do tons of TV, movie, and recording artists, authors, and people in the news.

The big chats of the day are often featured on the Welcome Screen. You can also check the full schedule at **Keyword: Live.**

Love@AOL

Finding love online is fun, free, and it works!
It's estimated that as many as 8,000 couples who
met on AOL have gone on to marry. The success
stories are amazing. Again and again, we hear
from people who have found the love of their lives
without ever braving the "bar scene."

It's no wonder "digital dating" has gone main-
stream. Every day on Love@AOL, (**Keyword:
Love**), thousands of people who might not otherwise have met— maybe because they don't live
near each other or "don't get out enough"—meet
and communicate online. Love@AOL provides the
perfect forum to mingle and get to know people
at your own convenience and pace.

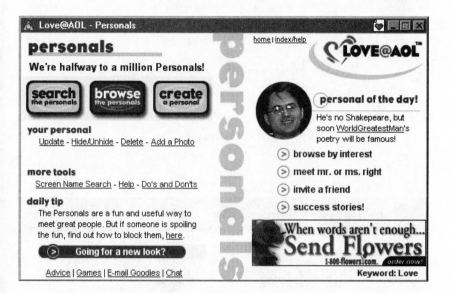

There are more than 500,000 personals posted on Love@AOL, including the largest collection of photo personals anywhere in cyberspace. They're easy to browse. If you'd like to create your own personal, just follow the directions. It takes a matter of minutes, but remember: the information is public, so don't post personal information like your home address or telephone number.

Importantly, if you meet someone special online and decide to take your relationship to the next level and meet in-person, take it slowly and use common sense. For example, be sure to meet in a public place and consider taking a few friends along to make it a "double date" or a group outing.

Music

You can turn your computer into a radio or CD player. With AOL 6.0 you can play music and run music videos with the click of a button. Check it out at **Keyword: Music.**

The Games Channel

The AOL Games channel, as you might guess from its name, is another prime source of online fun. You can play everything from simple card games to complex sci-fi action games. **Keyword: Games.** You should be aware that there is a premium charge for some games. It's also worth noting that the Games channel displays ratings providing information about both the age-appropriateness and content of each game.

Slingo

Slingo is a game you can play only on AOL—and it's quickly become one of the most popular areas online. The best way to describe it is as a combination of bingo and a slot machine game, but the best way to learn about Slingo is to take a look. Enter **Keyword: Slingo** to get to the main Slingo page.

The first time you play, you'll need to download the game, which may take a little while (as long as half an hour, depending on your modem speed and other factors), but after that, you'll never need to do so again. To download, go to the Slingo page and click on "Public Slingo" (Private Slingo—which lets you set up special games with your friends and families—costs extra). At the next page that comes up, click "Play Slingo" and a smaller window will come up asking you if you want to download the game. Click "OK" and you're on your way (this is the part that will take a little while).

Once the download is completed, the Slingo game screen will appear. Now you're ready to play!

You're also ready, as you can see, to chat. The chat window above the game board works just like the chat rooms we learned about on Day 2. Lots of people enjoy conversing with their fellow players while the game is in progress.

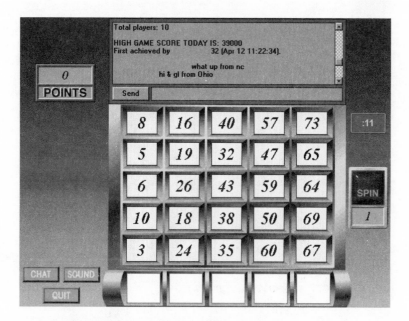

You might also consider checking out a classic game. Go to **Keyword: Solitaire.**

INSIDER TIPS

→ If you miss a scheduled chat, fear not; transcripts are often posted on AOL Live. **Keyword: Live.**

→ If you have questions about playing Games, there are eight steps to Mastering Online Games, outlining how to get started. **Keyword: How To.**

→ Based on AOL member feedback, photo personals are generally more effective than those without, so it's worth taking time to include a picture if you can. Step by step instructions are posted on Love@AOL. **Keyword: Love.**

Hi-Wired

Fantasy Sports

One of the fastest
growing hobbies
among sports fans
is fantasy sports
leagues. At the
beginning of the
real-life baseball,
football, basketball,
or whatever season,
people choose their favorite
players and pick teams. As the season

goes on, they follow how those players do, and get points based on different statistics (home runs in baseball, or points in basketball, or tackles in football, etc.). The person whose players did the best at the end of the season wins.

AOL makes playing in fantasy leagues easy. You can check in every day for updates about how your team and your opponents' teams are doing. You can also get all kinds of advice from sports experts.

Different sports will work differently, but check **Keyword: Fantasy Sports** in the months before your favorite sports season starts for more information on how to get started.

DAY 7

Get a (Family) Life

One of the best things about AOL is sharing it with your kids, as a means of having fun together and as a tool to help them learn. How early can your child start to enjoy the online experience? I used to check my e-mail every morning with my infant daughter in my lap. To this day, when you ask her where her mom works, she doesn't say "America Online"—she says, "You've Got Mail!"

Indeed, there are more kids online than ever and they're coming online at younger and younger ages. Twenty-five percent of recently polled AOL parents say their children are coming online as early as age two, with that number climbing to 90% by age six. If you have young people in the house, you probably won't be surprised by the fact that AOL parents also report their children are more likely to "fight" over the computer than the telephone. The online medium is really their medium and all indications are today's young people will grow up in an increasingly "connected" society.

A recent study of parents with children online indicated that most felt it had positive results. 71% said it had improved the quality of their children's homework, 70% said it had a positive effect on their children's skills for entering the job market someday, 64% said it had enhanced the quality of their children's overall written communication, and 56% said it had increased their children's interest in hobbies.

At the same time, a lot of parents worry about letting their kids go online, which is why AOL offers Parental Controls. **Keyword: Parental Controls**. These let you control the content your children can access, whether or not they're allowed to use e-mail and instant messaging, and even how much time they spend online. Having said that, there's no substitute for direct parental involvement. Ask your kids: "What are your favorite online places?" "Who are your online friends?" It's just like wanting to know where they are after school and whom they're hanging out with. No parent can be there every minute of every day. Parental Controls puts the power in the parents' hands where it belongs, while ensuring your children are getting all the advantages of the online world while minimizing its hazards.

Let's Do It

Setting Up Parental Controls

The first step is to set up a screen name for your child. Go to **Keyword: "Screen Name"** and click where it says "create a name." A box will come up asking you whether this name is for a child under 18. Click yes, if appropriate, and a message will appear explaining some of AOL's online privacy and security policies for children. Take a few minutes to review them.

After you're done, click "continue," and onscreen directions will guide you through the same process of choosing a screen name that you went through for yourself. At the end of that process, you will be asked whether you wish to designate this as a "master screen name." If the account is for your child, be sure to click "no," so that he or she will not be able to alter the parental controls settings you pick.

Once you've finished setting up the screen name, you're ready to set up parental controls.

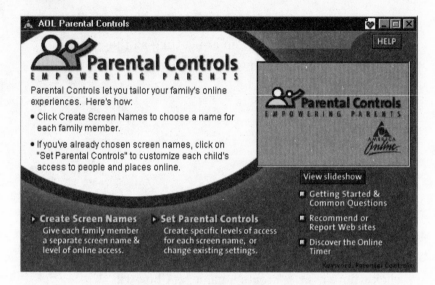

Sign on to the first screen name you created.
(This is called the "master" screen name.) Go to
Keyword: Parental Controls. First choose your

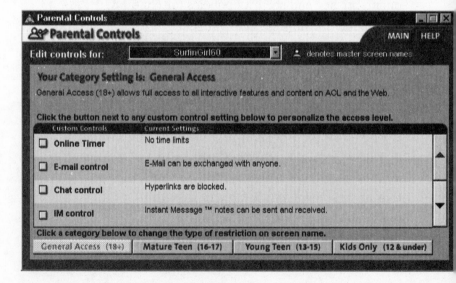

child's screen name from the box at the top of the
screen. Click on "Set Parental Controls." This will
connect you to a menu of choices.

The box in the middle of the screen lets you
customize the settings you choose for your kids.
Most people prefer to choose one of the standard
settings at the bottom of the screen for their
child's age group:

- ☞ *Kids Only (12 & under)* allows access only
  to age-appropriate interactive features,
  chat rooms, and content through AOL's
  Kids Only channel and the Web.
- ☞ *Young Teen (13–15)* allows access to age-
  appropriate interactive features and content on AOL and the Web. Access to
  Premium services, private and member-
  created chat rooms, and instant message
  notes are blocked.
- ☞ *Mature Teen (16–17)* allows access to
  most interactive features and content on
  AOL and the Web. Web sites and news-
  groups with explicitly mature content are
  blocked. Premium services are blocked.

You can choose any of these settings by simply
clicking on the appropriate box.

If you want to alter parts of these settings to
customize them as you think appropriate, click on

the setting in question and read the options care-fully. Select the one you want by clicking on the circle next to it. Then click "OK."

One specific item you may want to set is our AOL-exclusive online timer feature, which lets you specify what hours of the day children are allowed on AOL, and how many hours a week you want them to spend online. For example, parents can set the timer so their children can spend two hours online every evening, except Wednesday, which is set aside for piano practice.

When you are done setting controls, you can click the menu screen closed and your changes will be saved.

Exploring with Your Kids Online

For young kids under age six. Start early—there are offerings on America Online for children as young as two. So if you've got young children or grandchildren, nieces or nephews, place them on your lap and explore. The AOL Families channel features "lapware" —it's called "lapware" because you're meant to put your child on your lap and experience it together. On the most basic level it's about spending time with your kids. They'll be thrilled by the sounds and colors. Go to the Families channel or **Keyword: Families**. It's that easy. And you'll be surprised by what they pick up.

Kids ages 6 to 12. There's an AOL just for kids. It's called Kids Only and it's free with your AOL subscription. From dinosaur clubs to the ability to create comic books, AOL Kids Only

gives young people ages 6 to 12 the age-appropriate content they want and parents the peace of mind they need. **Keyword: Kids**.

Teens. It used to be that kids came home from school or for the summer and picked up the telephone. Now they race to the computer. Teens are some of the most active AOL users. But you need to be sure their activities are suitable for their age. Again, be involved. Spend time together at the computer. These days most teens are pretty tech-savvy, so odds are you'll learn a thing or two and they'll get a kick out of showing you. Teens—help out the adults! **Keyword: Teens.**

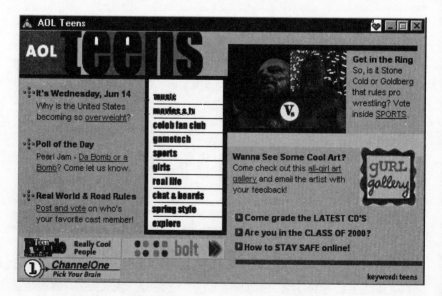

Homework Help

One of the most useful features
AOL offers for kids is our free
Ask-a-Teacher
function, where
volunteer real-
life teachers
are standing by
to help. On AOL,
we get over 13,000
questions a day!

Your kids can access
this assistance through the
Homework Help areas on
either the Kids Only or Teens
channels, or by going to **Keyword: Ask-a-Teacher** and selecting their
appropriate grade level from the menu.

For each grade level, there are several subject
areas—math, history, etc.—along with message
boards where children can post their questions
and check back later for help finding the
answers.

The high school Ask-a-Teacher section even
features live help in special chat rooms set up by
subject area. Students just click on the "Live
teacher help" button on the High School menu
to get to these chats, which are open on week-

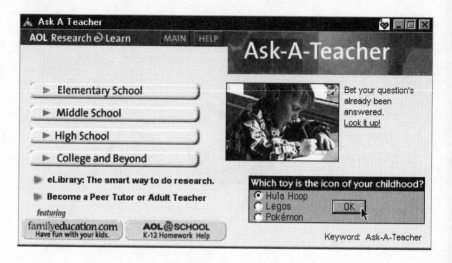

day and weekend evenings. For additional resources on a wide range of educational opportunities for young people and adults, go to **Keyword: Campus**. And don't forget about the always handy **Keyword: Dictionary, Keyword: Atlas,** and **Keyword: Thesaurus.**

INSIDER TIPS FOR PARENTS

→ Consider putting the computer in a central location such as the kitchen or the family room, where you can more easily swing by the screen and keep tabs on your children's online activities. Also, place a bench in front of the computer so it's easy to log on together with your children.

→ The online medium also makes it easier to give back. On the help-ing.org site (**Keyword: Helping**), you can find information about, and donate to, your favorite charities. There are also volunteer opportunities for the whole family.

→ America Online offers schools a free, education-focused program called AOL@School to help them make the most of the online medium as a tool for classroom learning. If your child's school has not signed up, urge them to call us at 1-888-468-3768 to get more information.

AOL@SCHOOL

→ Hometown: Building a homepage is a great way to keep friends and family updated, and it's terrific fun. Many people create home-pages with wedding and baby pictures. **Keyword: Hometown.**

Special Tips for Grandparents

One of the best ways to keep in touch with your grandchildren is to go to one of the places they are most—online! Exchanging e-mails can be a terrific way to stay in close contact and ask the questions you want to know most: How's school, soccer, camp? The online medium bridges distance and ages and is bringing families worldwide closer together.

Also, researching your family background is an adventurous and educational online activity to do with your grandchildren. Tracing your roots has never been easier. Search hundreds of genealogical databases, get valuable tips and

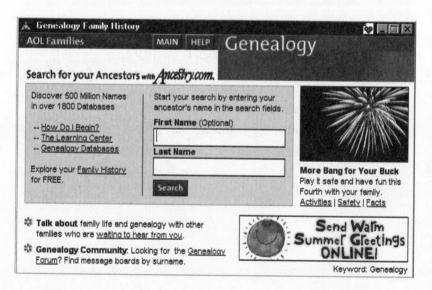

information on how to do research, and make your own contribution to the Ancestry World Tree. **Keyword: Genealogy.**

You've Got Pictures

Kids grow up so fast—everybody always wants to see the latest pictures. If my parents could see new pictures of my son and daughter every day, they'd be thrilled (and still want more!). Now AOL makes sharing pictures online as easy as e-mail.

World's Best Dog

Next Picture ►

It starts when you get film developed. Look for the AOL logo on the film processing envelope. Fill in your AOL e-mail address, and in a few days when you log in you'll hear a new announcement: "Welcome, You've Got Pictures!"

To see how they turned out, click on the "You've Got Pictures" icon on the Welcome Screen, then click "View" and use the scroll bar on the right-hand side of the screen to check out all of the pictures. If you like what you see, you can either send a single picture to anyone online in an e-mail, or create an album with multiple pictures to share.

Keeping Your Online Neighborhood Safe

Like anyplace else, the online world has a few dark corners. AOL works very hard to protect our members from online scams and other potential hazards, but we urge you to do your part as well. A lot of this comes down to common sense—knowing who you're dealing with—and using the features that AOL has built to allow you to control your online experience. To this end, here's some good advice.

E-mail Safety Tips

☞ *Use Mail Controls to block junk e-mail.*
As the Internet world grows, so do the
problems of junk e-mail—unsolicited,
unwelcome e-mail. In addition to our ongo-
ing efforts to block this unwelcome e-mail,
there are some simple things that you can
do too:

☞ *Official AOL Mail.* Determine if an e-mail
is Official AOL Mail by looking for a blue
envelope in your mailbox, a blue border
around the mail and the "Official AOL Mail"
seal. Go to **Keyword: Official AOL Mail**
to learn more.

☞ *Set Mail Controls.* With the Mail Controls
feature, you can control the e-mail you and
your children receive. You can also block
specific screen names or Internet
addresses from sending you mail. You can
also block the exchange of mail with
attached files or pictures. For more information, go to **Keyword: Mail Controls.**

☞ *Don't take hyperlinks or attachments from
strangers.* Online scam artists will often
send people hyperlinks or attachments that
they claim are official AOL instructions,

special offers, or the like. Don't believe them. If you get e-mail from someone you don't know with a hyperlink in it, don't click on it. If it has an attachment you're not expecting, don't download it. These are sometimes tricks used to spread computer viruses that could harm your computer or invade your personal privacy.

 ## Additional Safety Tips

☞ Don't give your AOL password to just anyone. It's fine to give out your screen name (e-mail address). Kids should not give out their screen names without their parents' permission.

☞ Create a different screen name for chat rooms and if you post an online personal. Go to **Keyword: Screen names**, and click "Create a screen name." Refer to Day 1 for more details on this.

☞ Select a password that combines letters and numbers. **Keyword: Password** has more information on creating secure passwords.

☞ Use different passwords for each screen name on your account.

☞ Report all offending e-mail to screen name TOSEmail1 or by using **Keyword: Notify AOL**.

 ## Safety Tips—for Kids

☞ Don't give your AOL password to anyone, even your best friend, brother, or sister.

☞ Never tell anyone your home address, telephone number, or school name without your parent's permission first. Don't type this information into a Web page online either, without checking with your parents.

☞ If someone says something that makes you feel unsafe or funny, don't respond to them. Tell your parents and AOL. Find out how at **Keyword: Kid Help.**

☞ Never say you'll meet someone in person without asking your parents' permission.

☞ Don't accept things from strangers (e-mail, files, Web page addresses, hyperlinks).

Keyword: Neighborhood Watch has more information on all of these topics.

Congratulations: You're wired!

I hope this book is only the beginning of your online journey. There's plenty more to learn about the constantly expanding world of the Internet. We're always adding to and updating the AOL Service. The best way to stay on top of what's new is to keep on exploring. You'll find even more features and areas designed to make your life easier and more convenient.

On behalf of everyone at America Online, thanks for taking the time to use this book, and here's looking forward to connecting with you again soon.

Enjoy!
Regina Lewis

Feedback: We want to hear from you about what you find helpful about this book, and what you'd like to know more about. Visit **Keyword: Wired in a Week** and tell us what you think.

The AOL Toolbar . . .

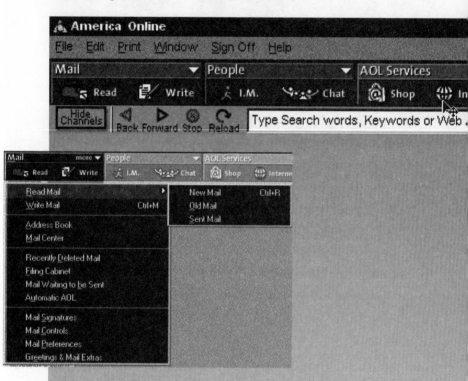

Index